Masterworks for Violin

Four Virtuoso Showpieces

for Unaccompanied Violin
Works by ERNST, LOCATELLI & VECSEY

Edited by Endre Granat

Contents

KEISER®

PREFACE

Four Virtuoso Showpieces for Unaccompanied Violin

Heinrich Wilhelm Ernst (1812-1865) was a brilliant violinist, violist, chamber musician and composer. In his compositions, he combined Paganini's technical innovations (harmonics, double harmonics, pizzicato and use of the entire range of the instrument) with a more sophisticated and advanced compositional style.

The Last Rose of Summer is a set of 4 Variations and Finale on a traditional Irish tune. This work is part of Ernst's *Polyphonic Etudes* for violin.

The Erlkönig (King of the Alders) is based on the famous lied by Schubert, not a transcription but a *tour de force* of innovative composing for violin.

Pietro Antonio Locatelli (1695-1764) was a violinist and composer of virtuoso violin music. His *12 Concertos, Op. 3* with their *24 Caprices* set the technical standard for virtuoso violinists. The unaccompanied *Caprices* were meant to be exercise pieces aimed at mastering the difficulties of the concertos.

Labyrinth is a treasure trove of studies of double stops, chords, arpeggios, trills, harmonics and various bowings, but most of all unusually wide stretches. Locatelli's works have greatly influenced Paganini's writing, especially in his *24 Caprices*.

Franz von Vecsey (1893-1935) was a veritable child prodigy. By age 10, he was considered one of the finest violinists in Europe. For a while, Bela Bartok was his piano accompanist. At age 12, he received the dedication of the Sibelius *Violin Concerto*, which he performed the following year. Vecsey dedicated the *Preludio e Fuga* in C minor to his teacher, Jenö Hubay.

Endre Granat, Editor

THE LAST ROSE OF SUMMER

Edited by
Endre Granat

HEINRICH WILHELM ERNST

Violin

Andante non troppo

Violin

Violin

Var. II

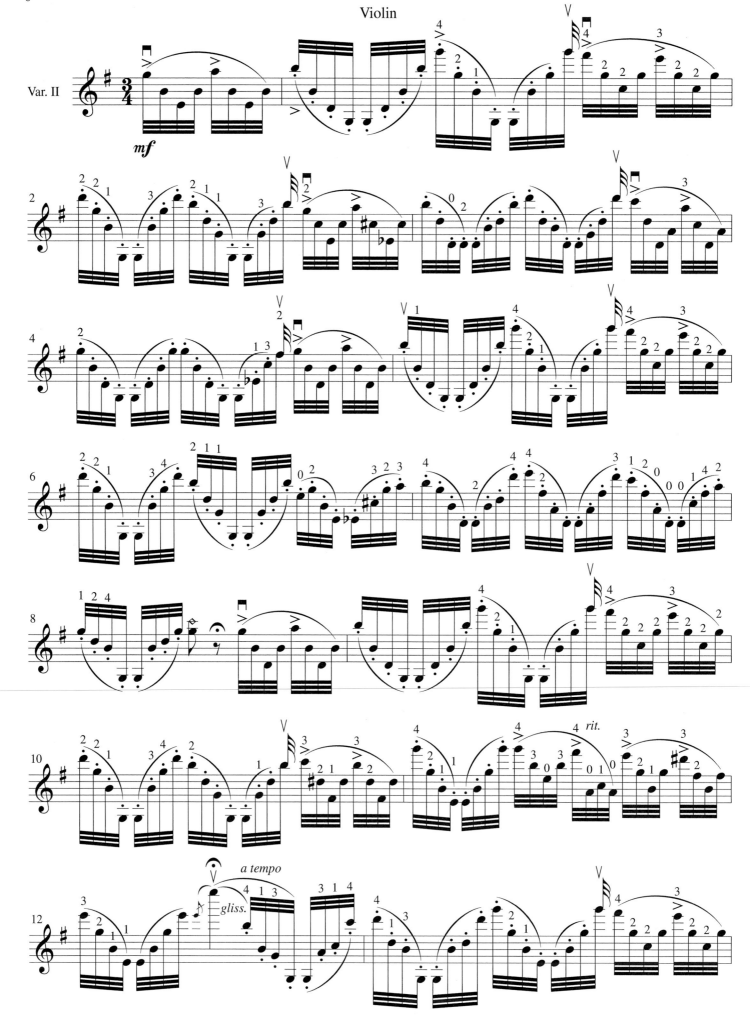

Violin

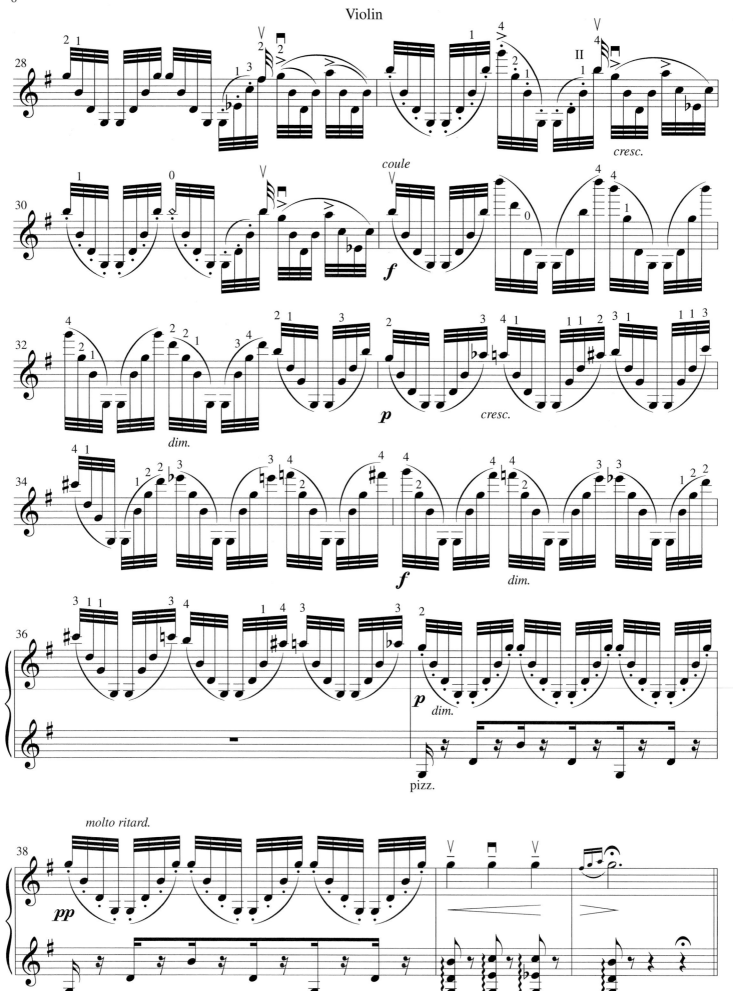

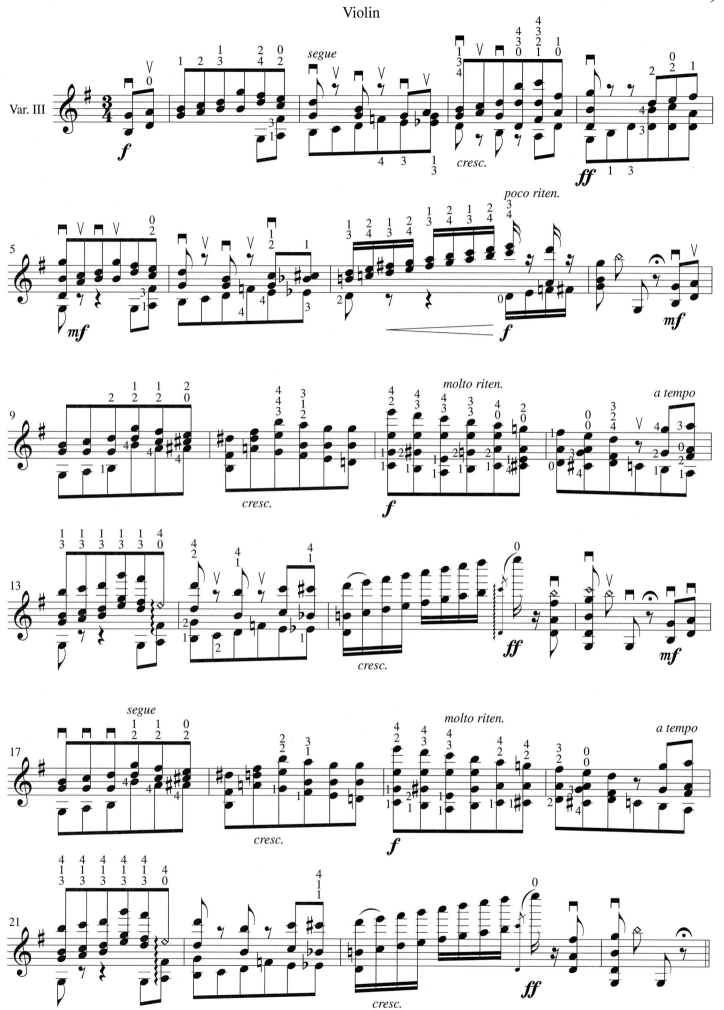

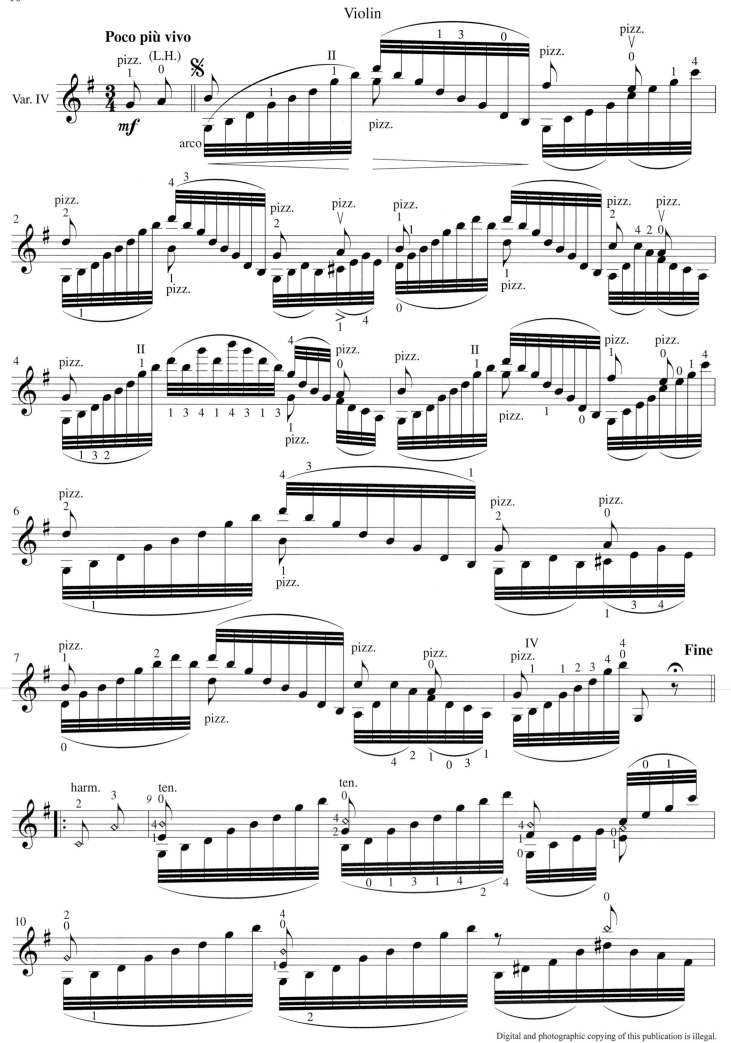

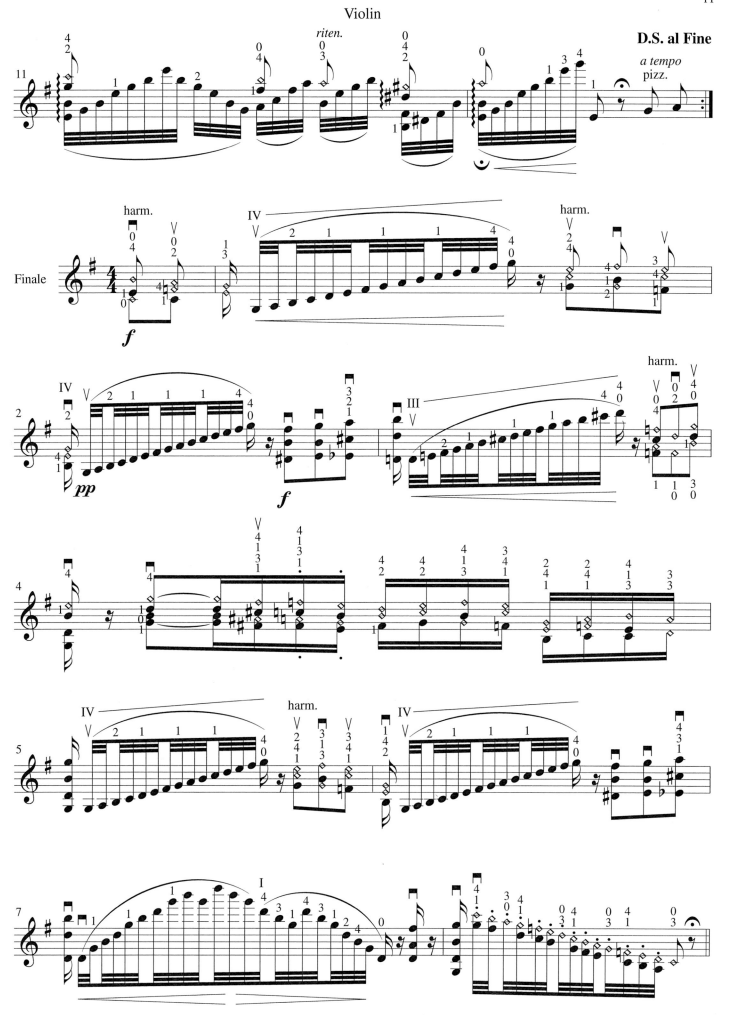

Violin

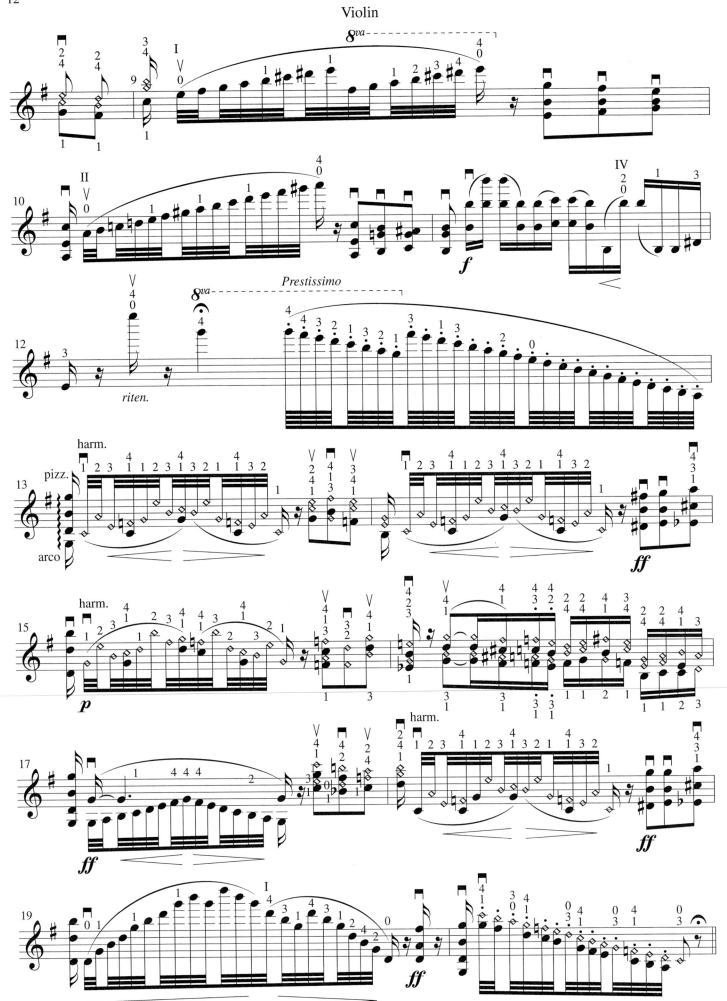

Violin

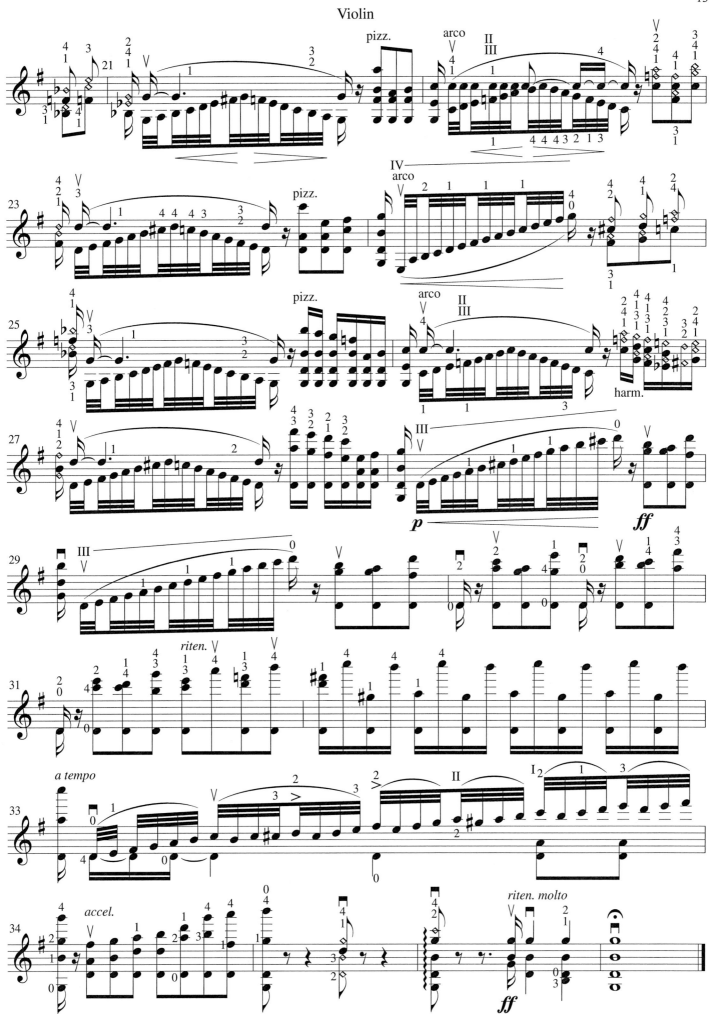

ERLKÖNIG
Grand Caprice after Schubert

Edited by
Endre Granat

HEINRICH WILHELM ERNST
Op. 26

Violin

Violin

Violin

Violin

LABYRINTH

Edited by
Endre Granat

PIETRO ANTONIO LOCATELLI
Op. 3/23

Violin

Violin

Violin

Violin

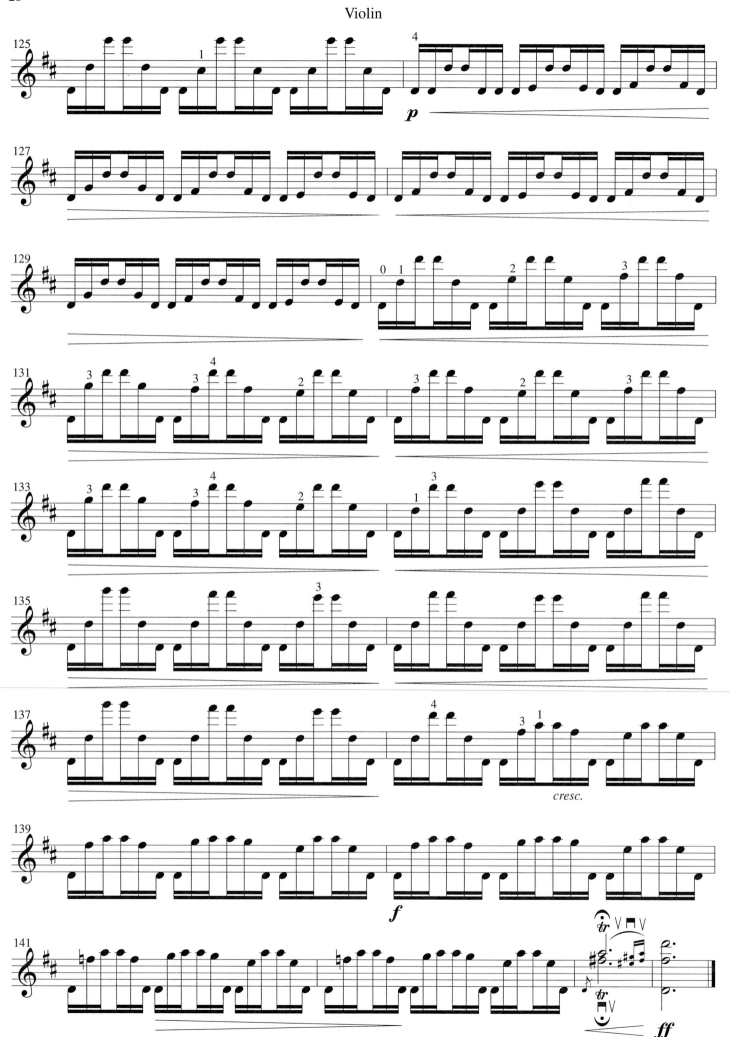

About the Editor

Endre Granat has studied with Zoltan Kodaly, Gyorgy Ligeti and Jascha Heifetz and is the premier concertmaster for the Hollywood film industry. He has performed with legendary conductors George Szell, Sir Georg Solti and Zubin Mehta. He is a Laureate of the Queen Elizabeth International competition and recipient of the Grand Prix du Disque and the Ysaye Medal.

PRELUDIO E FUGA

Edited by
Endre Granat

FRANZ VON VECSEY

*probably A♭

Violin

Violin

34

Violin

Violin